SCARVES, etc

4

13 KNITS FROM QUINCE & CO

Quince & Company, Inc
quinceandco.com

ISBN 978-0-9852990-7-1

Printed in the United States

TABLE OF CONTENTS

Introduction 6

Strix Varia .... 8 / 44

Torno .... 12 / 46

90-Degrees .... 14 / 50

Aviary .... 16 / 52

Sankaku .... 18 / 54

Pathway .... 20 / 58

Linda .... 22 / 60

Pomaika`i .... 26 / 62

Baroque .... 28 / 64

Inverness .... 30 / 68

Svalbard .... 34 / 70

Wending .... 36 / 72

Twist of Fate .... 38 / 76

Patterns 42

Abbreviations 80

Designer bios 82

Acknowledgements 88

Every year we ask knitters at large to submit their best scarf ideas for our on-line collection of favorite picks, *Scarves, etc*. Because these patterns are especially popular, this year we decided to make *Scarves, etc* not just a virtual collection, but a real hold-it-in-your-hands book, as well.

Why scarves (and cowls and shawls)? Ask any knitter and chances are she/he will tell you that her/his first project was a scarf. Scarves are a knitter's comfort project. They're simple and straightforward to knit (most of the time), and they also represent freedom and empowerment. Getting gauge isn't a deal breaker. In fact, you could easily start on suggested needles and yarn and even if you're off on the numbers, you'll still create an enviable piece. Scarves are easy to alter. Want it longer? Work more rows. Want it wider, cast on more stitches. And they're easy to invent for anyone with a stitch dictionary. Swatch a pattern in your favorite yarn and you're almost ready to cast on.

What I enjoy about this project is seeing the ways that knitters take a simple shape—rectangle, ring, triangle—and make it their own. For example:

Angela Tong's *Pathway* is a scarf embellished with classic knit/purl patterns that you'd find in a sailor's gansey. What makes the scarf not quite the usual is that she's arranged the patterns asymmetrically, a simple manipulation of a traditional idea. She's worked the scarf long for looping the neck more than once. In a bright poppy red, the scarf is very unworkman-like.

Katherine Mehls took our chunky Puffin yarn and doubled it for her cozy cowl, *90-Degrees*. No fancy stitch work here, just utilitarian fisherman rib scaled way up. For a tweak, she picked up and added a short band of the same rib that runs counter to the body of the cowl.

Aviary, Noriko Ho's drapey cowl, is ingenious. It's worked in a silk/wool blend that's fine enough to lend itself to layering. The top piece is a perforated lace pattern that allows a peek at the lining below, worked in a different color.

Michael Dworjan took a cable pattern from Barbara Walker's ever-inspiring *Treasury of Knitting Patterns* and based his technique, Keyhole Cables, on its twists and turns.

And so on.

This collection of scarves, cowls, and shawls, iconic knitted pieces meant to be utilitarian as well as pretty, showcases the many ways to invent something unusual and lovely with familiar stitches. We hope they will inspire you to knit them yourself, in your favorite color and, perhaps, adding your own tweak or two. So many ways to explore the possibilities sitting right there in your knitting basket.

Pam Allen

STRIX VARIA

by Shannon Squire

STRIX VARIA (CONT)

yarn: owl
colors: abyssinian
barents sea
yucca

TORNO

by Amy Maceyko

yarn: chickadee
color: damson

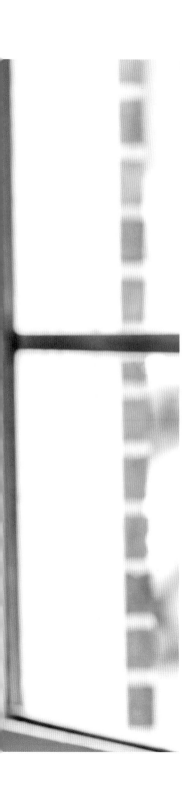

90-DEGREES

by Katherine Mehls

yarn: puffin
color: slate

AVIARY

by Noriko Ho

yarn: tern
colors: driftwood
dusk

SANKAKU

by Makiho Negishi

yarn: finch
color: bird's egg

PATHWAY
by Angela Tong

yarn: lark
color: poppy

LINDA
by Deb Hoss

LINDA (CONT)

yarn: lark
color: aleutian

POMAIKA`I

by Melissa Schoenwether

yarn: chickadee
color: barolo
      lichen

BAROQUE,
JANUS STYLE

by Michael Dworjan

yarn: chickadee
color: twig

INVERNESS

by Ellie Sokolow

INVERNESS

yarn: osprey
colors: slate
iceland
honey
poppy

SVALBARD

by Allison Jane

yarn: puffin
color: sedum

WENDING

by Quenna Lee

yarn: owl
color: abyssinian

TWIST OF FATE

by Laura Reinbach

TWIST OF FATE (CONT.)

yarn: chickadee
color: clay

PATTERNS

STRIX VARIA SHAWL

Shannon Squire

Strix Varia is the scientific name for the Barred Owl, the ubiquitous Hoot Owl native to North America. This comfy and cozy shawlette has a woody texture, wide wingspan, and lovely interplay of colors, perfect for any pursuit, be it owl-watching or knitting while binge-watching Hulu Plus.

Finished measurements
64" [162.5 cm] wingspan and 19" [48.5 cm] long at center spine

Yarn
Owl by Quince & Co
(50% American wool, 50% alpaca; 120yd [110m]/50g)
- 1 skein Abyssinian 309 (A)
- 2 skeins Barents Sea 326 (B)
- 1 skein Yucca 317 (C)

Needles
- One 24-32" circular needle (circ) in US 8 [5 mm]

Or size to obtain gauge

Notions
- Stitch marker (m)
- Locking stitch marker
- Tapestry needle

Gauge
15 sts and 30 rows = 4" [10 cm] in garter stitch, after blocking.

Special abbreviations
yo (yarn over): Bring yarn between needles to the front, then over RH needle ready to knit the next st (1 st increased).
sl 1 wyif: Slip 1 st purlwise with yarn in front.
k1-tbl: Knit stitch through the back loop to twist st.
k2tog-tbl: Knit 2 sts together through the back loops (1 st decreased).

Garter stitch
Knit every row.

Helpful links
For instructions on the **long-tail cast on**, we like: www.knitty.com/ISSUEsummer05/FEATsum-05TT.html
For instructions on the **cable cast on**, we like: www.knitty.com/ISSUEsummer05/FEATsum-05TT.html

Notes
1. Shawl begins at center of back neck with a garter tab. Stitches are increased at the side edges and center spine every WS row, and at side edges only every RS row throughout shawl.
2. Although gauge isn't crucial, please note that any change in gauge will affect yardage requirements and finished measurements.
3. To help distinguish RS from WS in garter stitch, after working a few rows, place a locking stitch marker on the RS of shawl.

Shawl

Begin at center of neck

With A and using the long-tail cast on, loosely CO 2 sts. Do not join.

Begin garter stitch tab

First row: (RS) Knit.

Work in garter stitch for 3 more rows. Do not turn the work after the last row, turn tab 90 degrees clockwise, pick up and knit 1 st in between garter ridges along side edge, then turn tab 90 degrees clockwise again, and pick up and knit 2 sts in CO edge—5 sts on needle.

Next row: (RS) Knit.

Begin shawl increases

Next row inc row: (WS) K2, yo, place marker, k1, yo, k2 (2 sts inc'd)—7 sts.

Next row inc row: K2, yo, knit to last 2 sts, yo, k2 (2 sts inc'd)—9 sts.

Next row inc row: K2, yo, knit to marker (m), yo, slip marker (sl m), k1, yo, knit to last 2 sts, yo, k2 (4 sts inc'd)—13 sts.

Next row inc row: K2, yo, knit to last 2 sts, yo, k2 (2 sts inc'd)—15 sts.

Rep the last 2 rows ten more times—75 sts on needle.

Begin slip stripe pattern

Next row inc row: (WS) With B, k2, yo, (k1, sl 1 wyif) to 1 st before m, k1, yo, sl m, k1, yo, (k1, sl 1 wyif) to last 3 sts, k1, yo, k2 (4 sts inc'd)—79 sts.

Next row inc row: K2, yo, knit to last 2 sts, yo, k2 (2 sts inc'd)—81 sts.

Next row inc row: With A, k2, yo, (k1, sl 1 wyif) to 2 sts before m, k2, yo, sl m, k1, yo, k2, (sl 1 wyif, k1) to last 2 sts, yo, k2 (4 sts inc'd)—85 sts.

Next row inc row: K2, yo, knit to last 2 sts, yo, k2 (2 sts inc'd)—87 sts.

Rep the last 4 rows six more times—159 sts on needle.

Break A.

Begin garter section

Next row inc row: (WS) With B, k2, yo, knit to m, yo, sl m, k1, yo, knit to last 2 sts, yo, k2 (4 sts inc'd)—163 sts.

Next row inc row: K2, yo, knit to last 2 sts, yo, k2 (2 sts inc'd)—165 sts.

Rep the last 2 rows 11 more times—231 sts on needle.

Begin slip stripe pattern

Row 1 inc row: (WS) With C, k2, yo, (k1, sl 1 wyif) to 1 st before m, k1, yo, sl m, k1, yo, (k1, sl 1 wyif) to last 3 sts, k1, yo, k2 (4 sts inc'd)—235 sts.

Row 2 inc row: K2, yo, knit to last 2 sts, yo, k2 (2 sts inc'd)—237 sts.

Row 3 inc row: With B, k2, yo, (k1, sl 1 wyif) to 2 sts before m, k2, yo, sl m, k1, yo, k2, (sl 1 wyif, k1) to last 2 sts, yo, k2 (4 sts inc'd)—241 sts.

Row 4 inc row: K2, yo, knit to last 2 sts, yo, k2 (2 sts inc'd)—243 sts.

Rep the last 4 rows five more times—291 sts on needle.

Break B.

Begin garter section

Next row inc row: (WS) With C, k2, yo, knit to m, yo, sl m, k1, yo, knit to last 2 sts, yo, k2 (4 sts inc'd)—295 sts.

Next row inc row: K2, yo, knit to last 2 sts, yo, k2 (2 sts inc'd)—297 sts.

Rep the last 2 rows two more times—309 sts on needle.

Break C.

Next row inc row: (WS) With A, k2, yo, knit to m, yo, sl m, k1, yo, knit to last 2 sts, yo, k2 (4 sts inc'd)—313 sts.

Next row inc row: K2, yo, knit to last 2 sts, yo, k2 (2 sts inc'd)—315 sts.

I-cord trim

Next row: (WS) Work i-cord bind off as follows: Using the cable cast on, CO 2 sts, *k1-tbl, k2tog-tbl; rep from * until 2 sts rem. Break yarn and draw through rem sts.

Finishing

Weave in ends. Steam- or wet-block shawl to finished measurements.

TORNO COWL
Amy Maceyko

After being disappointed in an entrelac design that looked great on the right side but boring on the wrong side, I swatched to find a reversible entrelac pattern that would accentuate the directional quality of the technique. One-by-one rib has the advantage of working well in small squares, keeping the stockinette look of the project, and making a warm fabric. The cowl is big enough to be worn long or doubled up for extra warmth.

Finished measurements
48" [122 cm] circumference and 7" [18 cm] deep

Yarn
Chickadee by Quince & Co
(100% American wool; 181yd [166m]/50g)
• 3 skeins Damson 149

Needles
• One 40" circular needle in size US 3 [3.25 mm]

Or size to obtain gauge

Notions
• Stitch marker
• Locking stitch marker
• Tapestry needle

Gauge
32 sts and 36 rows = 4" [10 cm] in rib stitch, after blocking
Entrelac 9-stitch repeat = 2" [5 cm] wide, after blocking.

Special abbreviations
sl 1 wyib: Slip 1 st knitwise with yarn in back.
sl 1 wyif: Slip 1 st purlwise with yarn in front.
p2tog: Purl 2 sts together (1 st decreased).
ssk (slip, slip, knit): Slip 2 sts one at a time knitwise to the RH needle; return sts to LH needle in turned position and knit them together through the back loops (1 st decreased, leans to the left).

Rib stitch (for swatching, even number of sts)
Row 1: (RS) *K1, p1; rep from * to end.
Rep Row 1 every row for rib stitch.

Helpful links
For instructions on the **Channel Island cast on**, we like:
www.youtube.com/watch?v=up-0QOubXQ8

For instructions on the **knitted cast on**, we like:
www.knitty.com/ISSUEsummer05/FEATsum-05TT.html

Notes
1. Cowl is worked in the round using a technique called entrelac. Rows are built up in ribbed segments, alternating between right- and left-leaning sets. The cowl begins at the bottom, working ribbing in the round, then the base set of triangles is created by working the circumference of the cowl in 9-stitch segments, building up small triangles using short rows. Once the first round is achieved, stitches are picked up and knitted in the side edge of the first triangle and worked in a leaning rectangle decreasing the live stitches of the previous triangle one short row at a time. Stitches are picked up in each triangle edge, and each worked in a right-leaning rectangle, until you again reach the beginning of the round. Then stitches are picked up in the side edge of the first rectangle, and worked back in the same manner, creating a set of left-leaning rectangles leading back, again, to the beginning of the round. The rectangles are repeated, then a top triangle set is worked to prepare the stitches to work the top rib trim. Although the cowl is worked in the round, due to the nature of entrelac, the entire body of the cowl is worked back and forth in multiple series of short rows.
2. To help distinguish RS from WS in this reversible pattern, place a locking stitch marker on the RS of cowl in the ribbing before beginning entrelac.

Cowl

Using the Channel Island cast on, CO 216 sts. Place marker (pm) for beg of rnd (BOR) and join to work in the rnd, being careful not to twist sts.

Begin rib trim

First rnd: *K1, p1; rep from * to end.
Cont in rib as est until pc meas ¾" [2 cm] from beg.

Begin base triangles

Triangle 1

Next row *short row 1:* (RS) K1, turn work; (WS) p1, turn work—1 st in triangle.
Next row *short row 2:* (RS) Sl 1 wyib, p1, turn work; (WS) k1, p1, turn work—2 sts in triangle.
Next row *short row 3:* (RS) Sl 1 wyib, work in rib to 1 st past last turning point, turn work; (WS) work in rib to last turning point, turn work—3 sts in triangle.
Rep *short row 3* six more times—9 sts in triangle.
Next row: (RS) Sl 1 wyib, work in rib to last turning point. Do not turn work.

Triangle 2

Next row *short row 1:* (RS) P1, turn work; (WS) k1, turn work—1 st in triangle.
Next row *short row 2:* (RS) Sl 1 wyif, k1, turn work; (WS) p1, k1, turn work—2 sts in triangle.
Next row *short row 3:* (RS) Sl 1 wyif, work in rib to 1 st past last turning point, turn work; (WS) work in rib to last turning point, turn work—3 sts in triangle.
Rep *short row 3* six more times—9 sts in triangle.
Next row: (RS) Sl 1 wyif, work in rib to last turning point. Do not turn work.

Cont as est, alternating Triangles 1 and 2 to end—24 triangles on needle. Remove BOR marker.

Set up for right-leaning rectangles

With RS facing, pick up and knit 9 sts along side edge of first triangle worked in previous row. Pm for BOR.
Next row *short row set up:* (WS) Sl 1 wyif, (k1, p1) three times, k1, p2tog with next st on LH needle, turn work—9 sts.
Next row *short row:* (RS) Work in rib to last turning point, turn work; (WS) sl 1 wyif, (k1, p1) three times, k1, p2tog with next st on LH needle, turn work.
Rep the last short row seven more times to complete set up rectangle. All sts from previous triangle have been decreased. Do not turn work after last WS row.

Begin right-leaning rectangles

With WS facing, pick up and knit 9 sts purlwise along side edge of next triangle, place last picked up st onto LH needle and p2tog with next st on LH needle—9 sts.
Next row *short row:* (RS) (K1, p1) four times, k1, turn work; (WS) sl 1 wyif, (k1, p1) three times, k1, p2tog with next st on LH needle, turn work.
Rep the last short row seven more times to complete one right-leaning rectangle. Do not turn work after last WS row.

Cont as est, working right-leaning rectangles to end—24 right-leaning rectangles on needle. Remove BOR marker.

Set up for left-leaning rectangles

With WS facing, pick up and knit 9 sts purlwise along side edge of first rectangle worked in previous row. Pm for BOR.
Next row *short row set up:* (RS) Sl 1 wyib, (p1, k1) three times, p1, ssk with next st on LH needle, turn work.
Next row *short row:* (WS) (P1, k1) four times, p1, turn work; (RS) sl 1 wyib, (p1, k1) three times, p1, ssk with next st on LH needle, turn work.
Rep the last short row seven more times to complete set up rectangle. All sts from previous rectangle have been decreased. Do not turn work after last RS row.

Begin left-leaning rectangles

With RS facing, pick up and knit 9 sts knitwise along side edge of next rectangle, place last picked up st onto LH needle and ssk with next st on LH needle—9 sts.
Next row *short row:* (WS) (P1, k1) four times, p1, turn work; (RS) sl 1 wyib, (p1, k1) three times, p1, ssk with next st on LH needle, turn work.
Rep the last short row seven more times to complete one left-leaning rectangle. Do not turn work after last RS row.

Cont as est, working left-leaning rectangles to end—24 left-leaning rectangles on needle. Remove BOR marker.

Rep Set up for right-leaning rectangle, working into side edge of first rectangle worked in previous row, then work right-leaning rectangles to BOR.

Rep Set up for left-leaning rectangle, working into side edge of first rectangle worked in previous row, then work left-leaning rectangles to BOR.

Begin top triangles
Set up triangle
With RS facing, pick up and knit 9 sts along side edge of first rectangle worked in previous row. Pm for BOR.

Next row *short row set up:* (WS) (P1, k1) four times, p2tog with next st on LH needle, turn work.

Next row *short row 1:* (RS) Work in rib to 1 st before last turning point, turn work; (WS) (k1, p1) three times, k1, p2tog with next st on LH needle, turn work—8 sts rem.

Next row *short row 2:* (RS) Work in rib to 1 st before last turning point, turn work; (WS) (p1, k1) three times, p2tog with next st on LH needle, turn work—7 sts rem.

Next row *short row 3:* (RS) Work in rib to 1 st before last turning point, turn work; (WS) (k1, p1) two times, k1, p2tog with next st on LH needle, turn work—6 sts rem.

Next row *short row 4:* (RS) Work in rib to 1 st before last turning point, turn work; (WS) (p1, k1) two times, p2tog with next st on LH needle, turn work—5 sts rem.

Next row *short row 5:* (RS) Work in rib to 1 st before last turning point, turn work; (WS) k1, p1, k1, p2tog with next st on LH needle, turn work—4 sts rem.

Next row *short row 6:* (RS) Work in rib to 1 st before last turning point, turn work; (WS) p1, k1, p2tog with next st on LH needle, turn work—3 sts rem.

Next row *short row 7:* (RS) Work in rib to 1 st before last turning point, turn work; (WS) k1, p2tog with next st on LH needle, turn work—2 sts rem.

Next row *short row 8:* (RS) K1, turn work; (WS) p2tog with next st on LH needle—1 st rem. Do not turn work.

Triangle 1
With WS facing, pick up and knit 9 sts purlwise along side edge of next rectangle, place last picked up st onto LH needle and p2tog with next st on LH needle—9 sts.

Next row *short row 1:* (RS) (P1, k1) four times, turn work; (WS) (p1, k1) three times, p1, ssk with next st on LH needle, turn work—8 sts rem.

Next row *short row 2:* (RS) Work in rib to 1 st before last turning point, turn work; (WS) (k1, p1) three times, ssk with next st on LH needle, turn work—7 sts rem.

Next row *short row 3:* (RS) Work in rib to 1 st before last turning point, turn work; (WS) (p1, k1) two times, p1, ssk with next st on LH needle, turn work—6 sts rem.

Next row *short row 4:* (RS) Work in rib to 1 st before last turning point, turn work; (WS) (k1, p1) two times, ssk with next st on LH needle, turn work—5 sts rem.

Next row *short row 5:* (RS) Work in rib to 1 st before last turning point, turn work; (WS) p1, k1, p1, ssk with next st on LH needle, turn—4 sts rem.

Next row *short row 6:* (RS) Work in rib to 1 st before last turning point, turn work; (WS) k1, p1, ssk with next st on LH needle, turn work—3 sts rem.

Next row *short row 7:* (RS) Work in rib to 1 st before last turning point, turn work; (WS) p1, ssk with next st on LH needle, turn work—2 sts rem.

Next row *short row 8:* (RS) P1, turn work; (WS) ssk with next st on LH needle—1 st rem. Do not turn work.

Triangle 2
With WS facing, pick up and knit 9 sts purlwise along side edge of next rectangle, place last picked up st onto LH needle and p2tog with next st on LH needle—9 sts.

Next row *short row 1:* (RS) (K1, p1) four times, turn work; (WS) (k1, p1) three times, k1, p2tog with next st on LH needle, turn work—8 sts rem.

Next row *short row 2:* (RS) Work in rib to 1 st before last turning point, turn work; (WS) (p1, k1) three times, p2tog with next st on LH needle, turn work—7 sts rem.

Next row *short row 3:* (RS) Work in rib to 1 st before last turning point, turn work; (WS) (k1, p1) two times, k1, p2tog with next st on LH needle, turn work—6 sts rem.

Next row *short row 4:* (RS) Work in rib to 1 st before last turning point, turn work; (WS) (p1, k1) two times, p2tog with next st on LH needle, turn work—5 sts rem.

Next row *short row 5:* (RS) Work in rib to 1 st before last turning point, turn work; (WS) k1, p1, k1, p2tog with next st on LH needle, turn work—4 sts rem.

Next row *short row 6:* (RS) Work in rib to 1 st before last turning point, turn work; (WS) p1, k1, p2tog with next st on LH needle, turn work—3 sts rem.

Next row *short row 7:* (RS) Work in rib to 1 st before last turning point, turn work; (WS) k1, p2tog with next st on LH needle, turn work—2 sts rem.

Next row *short row 8:* (RS) K1, turn work; (WS) p2tog with next st on LH needle—1 st rem. Do not turn work.

Cont as est, alternating Triangles 1 and 2 to end. Remove BOR marker. With RS facing, sl 1 st wyif from RH to LH needle, wyib return st to RH needle, joining to work in the rnd.

Begin rib trim

Rnd 1: *K1, p1; rep from * to end.
Cont in rib as est for ¾" [2 cm].

Next rnd: Bind off all sts using the picot bind off as follows:

Using the knitted cast on, CO 2 sts. Pass the second st on LH needle over the first and off the needle two times, sl 1 st purlwise to RH needle, p1, then pass the second st on RH needle over the first and off the needle. *CO 2 sts, pass the second st on LH needle over the first and off the needle, sl 1 st purlwise to RH needle, then pass the second st on RH needle over the first and off the needle, p1, then pass the second st on RH needle over the first and off the needle; rep from * to end.

Finishing

Weave in ends. Steam- or wet-block cowl to finished measurements.

90-DEGREES COWL
by Katherine Mehls

I am a fool for a classic stitch such as Fisherman's Rib, but I like the idea of using it in an imaginative way. So I worked this cowl on a grand scale with two strands of Puffin and a big needle. The depth and texture of the fabric is oh, so satisfying!

Finished measurements
52" [132 cm] circumference and 8" [20.5 cm] deep

Yarn
Puffin by Quince & Co
(100% American wool; 112yd [102m]/100g)
- 4 skeins Slate 143 (yarn is held double)

Needles
- One 32" circular needle (circ) in size US 17 [12.75 mm]

Or size to obtain gauge

Notions
- Locking stitch marker
- Tapestry needle

Gauge
8½ sts and 16 rows = 4" [10 cm] in fisherman's rib held double, after blocking.

Special abbreviation
k1rb: Knit the next stitch in the row below.

Fisherman's rib (even number of sts)
Set up row: (WS) Purl.
Row 1: *P1, k1rb; rep from *, end p2.
Rep Row 1 every row for fisherman's rib.

Helpful links
For instructions on the **long-tail cast on**, we like:
www.knitty.com/ISSUEsummer05/FEATsum-05TT.html
For great instructions on **mattress stitch and seaming**, see:
www.knitty.com/ISSUEspring04/mattress.html

Notes
1. Cowl is worked flat lengthwise with double strand of yarn. Stitches are picked up along one long side, and rib pattern is worked for a few inches, then bound off. The short ends are joined using the mattress stitch.
2. When measuring row gauge, 2 rows of the pattern appear as 1 row. So, if you count 8 rows over 4" [10 cm], it's really 16 rows.
3. After working a few rows, place a locking stitch marker on the RS of piece to help distinguish RS from WS.

Cowl

With yarn held double and using the long-tail cast on, CO 12 sts. Do not join.

Begin at center back
Set up row: (WS) Work Set up row of fisherman's rib.
First row: (RS) Work Row 1 of patt.
Cont in patt until pc meas approx 52" [132 cm] from beg, ending after a WS row.
Next row: (RS) Bind off in p1, k1 rib, working last 2 sts as purl sts.

Begin trim
With RS facing, yarn held double, and beg at CO edge, pick up and knit 1 st in each garter ridge to BO edge. Total number of sts picked up must be an even number.

Set up row: (WS) Work Set up row of fisherman's rib.
First row: (RS) Work Row 1 of patt.
Work in patt as est for a total of 8 rows, ending after a WS row.
Next row: (RS) Loosely bind off in p1, k1 rib, working last 2 sts as purl sts.

Finishing
Weave in ends. Steam- or wet-block cowl to finished measurements.
With single strand of yarn, join CO and BO edges using the mattress stitch.

AVIARY COWL
Noriko Ho

Aviary Cowl is a fun and versatile pattern. I have a sweater with an open lacy back, and I was choosing a tank top to wear underneath it, when the idea for this layered cowl came to me. It can be knitted up in many different color combinations: muted and subtle as shown here, bright and bold, or bright lining with muted mesh, etc!

Finished measurements
54" [137 cm] circumference and 7½" [19 cm] deep

Yarn
Tern by Quince & Co
(75% American wool, 25% silk; 221yd [202m]/50g)
2 skeins each
- Dusk 415 (MC)
- Driftwood 401 (CC)

Needles
- Two 40" circular needles (circ) in size US 6 [4 mm]
- One spare needle in size US 7 [4.5 mm]

Or size to obtain gauge

Notions
- Waste yarn for invisible cast on
- Stitch marker (m)
- Tapestry needle

Gauge
23 sts and 34 rnds = 4" [10 cm] in stockinette stitch, before blocking
23 sts and 38 rnds = 4" [10 cm] in Irish mesh pattern, before blocking
20 sts and 38 rnds = 4" [10 cm] in stockinette stitch, after blocking
19 sts and 38 rnds = 4" [10 cm] in Irish mesh pattern, after blocking.

Special abbreviations
yo (yarn over): Bring yarn between needles to the front, then over RH needle ready to knit the next st (1 st increased).
sl 1: Slip 1 st purlwise with yarn in back.
psso2: Pass the slipped st over the 2 knit sts (1 st decreased).

Stockinette stitch (St st)
Knit every round.

Irish mesh pattern (multiple of 3 sts)
Rnd 1: *Yo, sl 1, k2, psso2; rep from * to end.
Rnd 2: Knit to last st, sl 1, remove marker (m), return st to LH needle, place marker (pm).
Rnd 3: *Sl 1, k2, psso2, yo; rep from *.
Rnd 4: Knit to end, remove m, k1, pm.
Rep Rnds 1-4 for Irish mesh pattern.

Techniques
Three-needle bind off
With WS together, hold the needles parallel. With a third needle, knit the first st of front and back needles together, *knit next st from each needle together (2 sts on RH needle), lift the first st over the second st and off the RH needle to BO 1 st; rep from * until all sts are bound off.

Helpful link
For instructions on the **invisible provisional cast on**, we like:
lucyintheskywithstitches.wordpress.com/2011/10/19/tutorial-invisible-provisional-cast-on

Notes
1. Cowl is knitted in the round, beginning with the lining (MC in stockinette stitch) followed by the overlay (CC in Irish mesh pattern). Then the piece is folded in half and joined using the three-needle bind off.
2. To maintain a continuous pattern, the beginning of round shifts by one stitch on even-numbered rounds.

Cowl

With circular needle (circ), using waste yarn and MC, and using the invisible provisional cast on, CO 270 sts.

Do not join.

Begin cowl lining
First row: (RS) With MC, knit.
Place marker (pm) for beg of rnd and join to work in the rnd, being careful not to twist sts.
Next rnd: Knit.
Cont in St st until pc meas 8" [20 cm] from beg.
Next rnd: With CC, knit.

Work turning rnd and begin cowl front
Next rnd *turning rnd*: Purl.
Next rnd: Knit.
Cont in St st until pc meas ½" [1.5 cm] from turning rnd.

Begin stitch pattern
Next rnd: Work Rnd 1 of Irish mesh pattern.
Cont in patt until pc meas 7½" [19 cm] from turning rnd.
Next rnd: Knit.
Cont in St st until pc meas 8" [20 cm] from turning rnd.
Weave in ends.

Close cowl
Remove waste yarn and place 270 sts from the provisional CO onto second circ. With WS together, fold cowl at turning rnd. With larger spare needle and using the three-needle bind off, BO all sts.

Finishing
Weave in remaining end. Steam- or wet-block cowl to finished measurements.

SANKAKU SHAWL
Makiho Negishi

Sankaku is the Japanese word for triangle. I got the inspiration from a classic Japanese motif.

Finished measurements
45" [114.5 cm] wingspan and 21" [53.5 cm] long at center spine

Yarn
Finch by Quince & Co
(100% American wool; 221yd [202m]/50g)
- 3 skeins Bird's Egg 106

Needles
- One 32" circular needle in size US 6 [4 mm]

Or size to obtain gauge

Notions
- Stitch markers (m)
- Tapestry needle
- Blocking wires and pins (optional)

Gauge
22 sts and 35 rows = 4" in triangle stitch, before wet-blocking
18 sts and 33 rows = 4" in triangle stitch, after wet-blocking.

Special abbreviations
yo (yarn over): Bring yarn between needles to the front, then over RH needle ready to knit the next st (1 st increased).

k2tog: Knit 2 sts together (1 st decreased, leans to the right).

ssk (slip, slip, knit): Slip 2 sts one at a time knit-wise to the RH needle; return sts to LH needle in turned position and knit them together through the back loops (1 st decreased, leans to the left).

s2kp (central double decrease): Slip 2 sts tog knitwise to the RH needle, k1, pass 2 slipped sts over knit st (2 sts decreased).

k2tog-tbl: Knit 2 sts together through the back loops (1 st decreased).

Triangle stitch (for swatching; multiple of 16 sts + 1)
Row 1: (RS) K2tog, *(yo, k2tog) three times, yo, k1, (yo, ssk) three times, yo, s2kp; rep from *, end (yo, k2tog) three times, yo, k1, (yo, ssk) four times.

Row 2 and all WS rows: Purl.

Row 3: K1, *(k2tog, yo) three times, k3, (yo, ssk) three times, k1; rep from *.

Row 5: K1, *k1, (k2tog, yo) three times, k1, (yo, ssk) three times, k2; rep from *.

Row 7: K1, *k2, (k2tog, yo) two times, k3, (yo, ssk) two times, k3; rep from *.

Row 9: K1, *k3, (k2tog, yo) two times, k1, (yo, ssk) two times, k4; rep from *.

Row 11: K1, *k4, k2tog, yo, k3, yo, ssk, k5; rep from *.

Row 13: K1, *k5, k2tog, yo, k1, yo, ssk, k6; rep from *.

Row 15: Knit.

Row 16: (RS) Purl.

Rep Rows 1-16 of triangle stitch for swatching.

Triangle stitch set up
See also chart, page 56.

Row 1: (RS) (Yo, k2tog) four times, yo, k1, (yo, ssk) four times, yo.

Row 2 and all WS rows: Purl.

Row 3: Yo, k2, (k2tog, yo) three times, k3, (yo, ssk) three times, k2, yo.

Row 5: Yo, k4, (k2tog, yo) three times, k1, (yo, ssk) three times, k4, yo.

Row 7: Yo, k6, (k2tog, yo) two times, k3, (yo, ssk) two times, k6, yo.

Row 9: Yo, k8, (k2tog, yo) two times, k1, (yo, ssk) two times, k8, yo.

Row 11: Yo, k10, k2tog, yo, k3, yo, ssk, k10, yo.

Row 13: Yo, k12, k2tog, yo, k1, yo, ssk, k12, yo.

Row 13: Yo, k12, k2tog, yo, k1, yo, ssk, k12, yo.
Row 15: Yo, knit to next m, yo.
Row 16: (WS) Purl.

Triangle stitch
See also chart, page 56.
Row 1: (RS) Yo, k2tog, *(yo, k2tog) three times, yo, k1, (yo, ssk) three times, yo, s2kp; rep from *, end (yo, k2tog) three times, yo, k1, (yo, ssk) four times, yo.
Row 2 and all WS rows: Purl.
Row 3: Yo, k2, *(k2tog, yo) three times, k3, (yo, ssk) three times, k1; rep from *, end k1, yo.
Row 5: Yo, k3, *k1, (k2tog, yo) three times, k1, (yo, ssk) three times, k2; rep from *, end k2, yo.
Row 7: Yo, k4, *k2, (k2tog, yo) two times, k3, (yo, ssk) two times, k3; rep from *, end k3, yo.
Row 9: Yo, k5, *k3, (k2tog, yo) two times, k1, (yo, ssk) two times, k4; rep from *, end k4, yo.
Row 11: Yo, k6, *k4, k2tog, yo, k3, yo, ssk, k5; rep from *, end k5, yo.
Row 13: Yo, k7, *k5, k2tog, yo, k1, yo, ssk, k6; rep from *, end k6, yo.
Row 15: Yo, knit to next m, yo.
Row 16: (WS) Purl.
Rep Rows 1-16 for triangle stitch.

Notes
1. Shawl is worked from the center of the neck out, beginning with a garter stitch tab. Increases are worked at each end and at center spine every RS row.
2. Wet-blocking (as opposed to steam-blocking) is recommended to achieve drape and proper gauge.

Shawl
Set up and work garter tab
Begin at center of neck, and using the long-tail cast on, loosely CO 6 sts. Do not join.
First row: (RS) Knit.
Knit 15 more rows. Do not turn the work after the last row, turn tab 90 degrees clockwise, pick up and knit 1 st in between garter ridges along side edge, then turn tab 90 degrees clockwise again, and pick up and knit 6 sts in CO edge—20 sts on needle.
Next row place markers: (WS) K6, place marker (pm), p1, pm, k6, pm, p1, pm, k6.

Set up for pattern
Row 1 inc row: (RS) *K6, slip marker (sl m), yo, knit to next marker (m), yo, sl m; rep from * one more time, knit to end (4 sts inc'd)—24 sts.
Row 2 and all WS rows: *Knit to m, purl to next m; rep from * one more time, knit to end.
Rep the last 2 rows seven more times—52 sts on needle.

Begin triangle set up
Row 1 inc row: (RS) *Knit to m, work Row 1 of triangle st set up to next m; rep from * one more time time, knit to end (4 sts inc'd)—56 sts.
Row 2 and all WS rows: *Knit to m, purl to next m; rep from * one more time, knit to end.
Cont as est, working through Row 16 of set up—84 sts on needle.

Begin triangle stitch pattern
Row 1 inc row: (RS) *Knit to m, work Row 1 of triangle st to next m; rep from * one more time, knit to end (4 sts inc'd)—88 sts.
Row 2 and all WS rows: *Knit to m, purl to next m; rep from * one more time, knit to end.
Cont as est, working Rows 1-16 of patt a total of four times—244 sts on needle.

Begin trim
Next row inc row: (RS) *Knit to m, sl m, yo, knit to next m, yo, sl m; rep from * one more time, knit to end (4 sts inc'd)—248 sts.
Next row: (WS) Knit.
Rep the last 2 rows five more times—268 sts on needle.
Next row: (RS) Work elastic bind off as follows: K1, *k1, return 2 sts to LH needle, k2tog-tbl; rep from * to end.

Finishing
Weave in ends. Wet-block shawl to finished measurements, using blocking wires and pins, if you like.

Triangle stitch set up

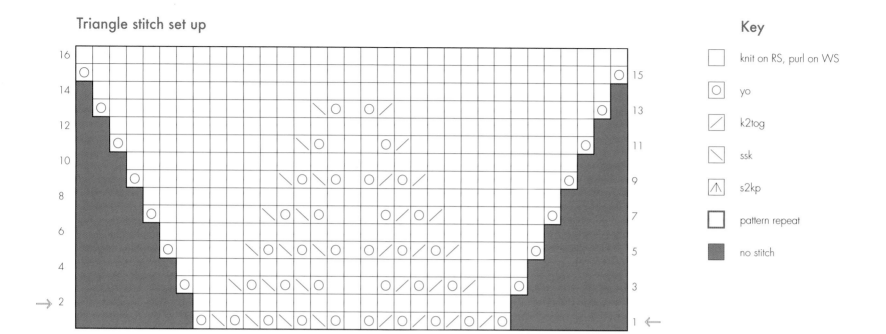

Key

☐	knit on RS, purl on WS
○	yo
╱	k2tog
╲	ssk
⋀	s2kp
☐	pattern repeat
�	no stitch

Triangle stitch

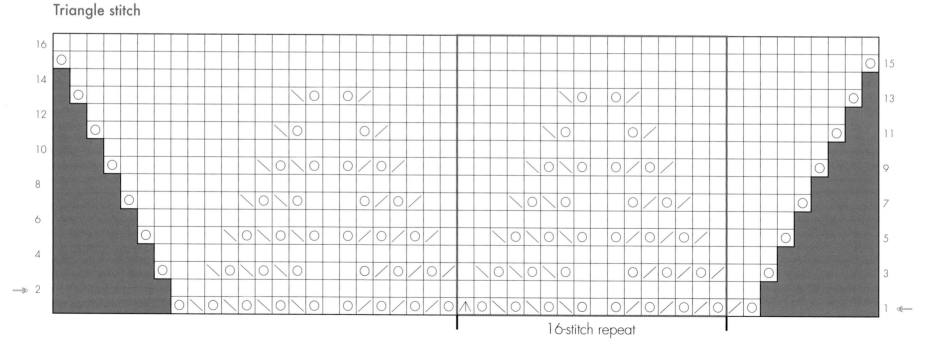

16-stitch repeat

Finished measurements
7¼" [18.5 cm] wide and 75" [190.5 cm] long

Yarn
Lark by Quince & Co
(100% American wool; 134yd [123m]/50g)
* 4 skeins Poppy 140

Needles
* One pair in size US 9 [5.5 mm]

Or size to obtain gauge

Notions
* Cable needle (cn)
* Tapestry needle
* Blocking wires and pins (optional)

Gauge
20 sts and 24 rows = 4" [10 cm] in stitch pattern, after blocking.

Special abbreviations
C4F (cable 4 front, leans to the left): Slip next 2 sts onto cable needle (cn) and hold in front, k2, then k2 from cn.

C4B (cable 4 back, leans to the right): Slip next 2 sts onto cn and hold in back, k2, then k2 from cn.

Stitch pattern (36 sts)
See also chart, next page.
Row 1: (RS) K3, p1, k2, p2, k8, p2, k4, p2, k3, p3, k2, p1, k3.
Row 2: (K1, p2) two times, k1, p1, k2, p3, k2, p3, k2, p8, k2, (p2, k1) two times.
Row 3: K3, p1, k2, p2, k8, p2, k2, p2, k3, p2, k2, p1, k2, p1, k3.
Row 4: (K1, p2) two times, k1, (p3, k2) two times, p1, k2, p8, k2, (p2, k1) two times.
Row 5: K3, p1, k2, p2, k8, p4, k3, p2, k4, p1, k2, p1, k3.
Row 6: (K1, p2) two times, k3, p3, k2, p3, k3, p8, k2, (p2, k1) two times.
Row 7: K3, p1, k2, p2, k8, (p2, k3) two times, p2, k1, p1, k2, p1, k3.
Row 8: (K1, p2) two times, k1, p2, k2, p3, k2, p2, k2, p8, k2, (p2, k1) two times.
Row 9: K3, p1, k2, p2, C4F, C4B, p2, k1, (p2, k3) two times, p1, k2, p1, k3.
Row 10: (K1, p2) two times, k1, p4, k2, p3, k4, p8, k2, (p2, k1) two times.
Rep Rows 1-10 for stitch pattern.

Helpful links
For instructions on the **long-tail cast on**, we like: www.knitty.com/ISSUEsummer05/FEATsum-05TT.html
For help on knitting **cables and cabling** without a cable needle, we like: www.knitty.com/ISSUEwinter07/FEATwin07TT.html

Note
Scarf is knitted in one piece lengthwise. Wet-blocking is recommended to maintain the cables.

PATHWAY SCARF
Angela Tong

Pathway is an easy to knit unisex scarf that looks great on everyone. The scarf features an asymmetrical arrangement of a cable and a diagonal stripe pattern bordered by ribbing. The 10-row stitch pattern is worked from one end to the other. Lark makes this scarf a quick knit and perfectly highlights this richly textured scarf.

Scarf

Using the long-tail cast on, CO 36 sts.

First row: (RS) Knit.
Next row: Knit.

Begin stitch pattern
Next row: (RS) Work Row 1 of stitch patt.
Cont in patt until pc meas approx 74½" [189 cm]
from beg, ending after Row 5.

Next row: (WS) Knit.
Next row: Knit.
Next row: Loosely bind off knitwise.

Finishing
Weave in ends. Wet-block scarf to finished measurements, using blocking wires and pins, if you like.

Stitch pattern

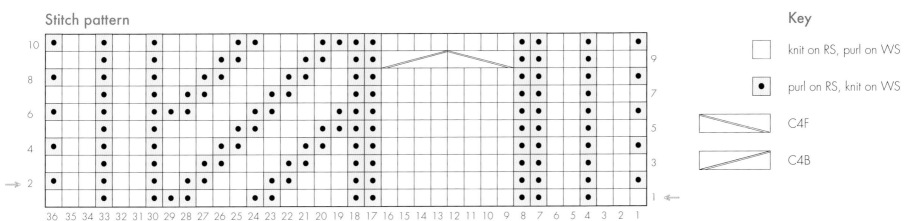

Key

☐	knit on RS, purl on WS
⊡	purl on RS, knit on WS
⟍	C4F
⟋	C4B

LINDA SCARF
Deb Hoss

Inspired by fringe! is the Linda scarf – generously long to loop around the neck and then some; textured with the reversible seeded rib check that keeps the knitter engaged; and fringed on its horizontal edges, an unexpected twist on a classic that's fun to do too.

Finished measurements
9" [23 cm] wide and 62" [157.5 cm] long with 2" [5 cm] fringe on each side

Yarn
Lark by Quince & Co
(100% American wool; 134yd [123m]/50g)
• 5 skeins Aleutian 148

Needles
• One pair in size US 8 [5 mm]
Or size to obtain gauge

Notions
• Stitch markers (m)
• Blocking wires and pins

Gauge
18½ sts and 28½ rows = 4" [10 cm] in seeded rib check, after blocking.

Seeded rib check (multiple of 4 sts +1)
See also chart, next page.
Rows 1, 3, and 5: (RS) P1, *k3, p1; rep from * eight more times.
Rows 2, 4, and 6: *K2, p1, k1; rep from * eight more times, k1.
Rows 7, 9, and 11: K1, *k1, p1, k2; rep from * eight more times.
Rows 8, 10, and 12: *P1, k3; rep from * eight more times, p1.
Rep Rows 1-12 for seeded rib check.

Helpful link
For instructions on the **long-tail cast on**, we like:
www.knitty.com/ISSUEsummer05/ FEATsum05TT.html

Note
Introduce yarn from new skeins at the beg of rows, where ends become part of the fringe and no weaving is required.

Scarf
Using the long-tail cast on, CO 55 sts.

Begin hem rib
Row 1 *place markers:* (RS) K5, (k1, p1) two times, place marker (pm), *k1, p1; rep from * to last 10 sts, k1, pm, (p1, k1) two times, k5.
Row 2: (WS) P5, (p1, k1) two times, slip marker (sl m), *p1, k1; rep from * to last 10 sts, p1, sl m, (k1, p1) two times, p5.
Rep these 2 rows two more times.

Begin seeded rib check
Next row: (RS) Work as est to marker (m), sl m, work Row 1 of seeded rib check to next m, sl m, work as est to end.
Next row: Work as est to m, sl m, work next row of patt to next m, sl m, work as est to end.
Cont in patt as est until pc meas approx 61" [155 cm], ending after Row 6.

Begin hem rib
Work Rows 1 and 2 of hem rib three times as indicated above, removing markers.
Next row: (RS) K5, BO 45 sts in rib patt, break yarn and draw tail through the last bound off st, then sl rem 5 sts off both needles.

Create fringe
Unravel the 5 unsecured sts on both sides of every row.

Finishing

Slip blocking wires into the curly loops of the unraveled sts on each side. Pull slightly to straighten yarn and align scarf body to meas, pin wires in place. Use spray bottle to dampen overall.

Once dry, leaving wires in place, trim fringe to 2" [5 cm] on each side.

Key

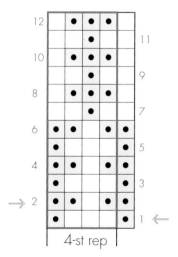

☐ knit on RS, purl on WS

▢• purl on RS, knit on WS

☐ pattern repeat

Seeded rib check

POMAIKA`I SHAWL

Melissa Schoenwether

Pomaika`i in Hawaiian means a blessing or good luck. Many years of my life were spent on the shores of a gentle grey beach drawing lines, one after the other, in the sand. To start and end one's day at the edge of the ocean is connecting and very central to island life on Kauai. The lines needed a way to be taken from the sand and my heart and yarn and needles recreated it in the shawl pattern you now have.

Finished measurements
53" [134.5 cm] wingspan and 22" [56 cm] long at center

Yarn
Chickadee by Quince & Co
(100% American wool; 181yd [166m]/50g)
- 3 skeins Barolo 146 (MC)
- 2 skeins Lichen 126 (CC)

Needles
- One 32" circular needle in size US 5 [3.75 mm]

Or size to obtain gauge

Notions
- Stitch marker
- Tapestry needle

Gauge
22 sts and 46 rows = 4" [10 cm] in garter stitch, after blocking.

Special abbreviation
k1-f/b (knit 1, front and back): Knit into the front loop, then the back loop of next st (1 st increased).

Garter stitch
Knit every row.

CC stripe pattern
Row 1: (RS) With MC, knit to 1 st before marker (m), with MC and CC held tog, k1, with CC, knit to end.
Row 2 inc row: With CC, k1-f/b, knit to m, with MC and CC held tog, k1, with MC, knit to end (1 st inc'd).

MC stripe pattern
Row 1: (RS) With MC, knit to 1 st before m, with MC and CC held tog, k1, with MC, knit to end.
Row 2 inc row: With MC, k1-f/b, knit to m, with MC and CC held tog, k1, with MC, knit to end (1 st inc'd).

Notes
1. Shawl begins in main color at left tip with increases on one edge to form a wide garter band. Increases continue as contrast color is introduced and continued in a random stripe, while maintaining the solid-colored band.
2. Increases occur every WS row.
3. Once the band is created and body of shawl begins, one stitch between band and body is worked in both main and contrast colors.

Shawl

Begin at left tip
With MC, make a slip knot and place on needle.

First row *inc row*: (WS) K1-f/b (1 st inc'd)—2 sts.
Next row: Knit.
Next row *inc row:* K1-f/b, knit to end (1 st inc'd)—3 sts.
Rep the last 2 rows 17 more times—20 sts on needle.
Next row: (RS) Knit.

Begin striped body and continue solid band
Next row *inc row:* (WS) K1-f/b, knit to end (1 st inc'd)—21 sts.
Next row *place marker:* K19, with MC and CC held tog, k1, place marker, with CC, k1.
Next row *inc row:* K1-f/b, slip marker (sl m), with MC and CC held tog, k1, with MC knit to end (1 st inc'd)—22 sts.
Next row: Work Row 1 of CC stripe patt.
Next row *inc row:* Work Row 2 of CC stripe patt—23 sts.
Rep the last 2 rows two more times—25 sts.

Next row: (RS) Work Row 1 of MC stripe patt.
Next row *inc row:* Work Row 2 of MC stripe patt—26 sts.
Rep the last 2 rows one more time—27 sts.

Work 6 rows in CC stripe patt—30 sts.
Work 12 rows in MC stripe patt—36 sts.
Work 2 rows in CC stripe patt—37 sts.
Work 4 rows in MC stripe patt—39 sts.
Work 4 rows in CC stripe patt—41 sts.
Work 2 rows in MC stripe patt—42 sts.
Work 6 rows in CC stripe patt—45 sts.

Work 4 rows in MC stripe patt—47 sts.
Work 2 rows in CC stripe patt—48 sts.
Work 2 rows in MC stripe patt—49 sts.
Work 10 rows in CC stripe patt—54 sts.
Work 4 rows in MC stripe patt—56 sts.
Work 4 rows in CC stripe patt—58 sts.
Work 8 rows in MC stripe patt—62 sts.
Work 10 rows in CC stripe patt—67 sts.
Work 14 rows in MC stripe patt—74 sts.
Work 2 rows in CC stripe patt—75 sts.
Work 4 rows in MC stripe patt—79 sts.
Work 16 rows in CC stripe patt—87 sts.
Work 2 rows in MC stripe patt—88 sts.
Work 4 rows in CC stripe patt—90 sts.
Work 6 rows in MC stripe patt—93 sts.
Work 12 rows in CC stripe patt—99 sts.
Work 10 rows in MC stripe patt—104 sts.
Work 10 rows in CC stripe patt—109 sts.
Work 4 rows in MC stripe patt—111 sts.
Work 4 rows in CC stripe patt—113 sts.
Work 6 rows in MC stripe patt—116 sts.
Work 4 rows in CC stripe patt—118 sts.
Work 2 rows in MC stripe patt—119 sts.
Work 8 rows in CC stripe patt—123 sts.
Work 16 rows in MC stripe patt—131 sts.
Work 6 rows in CC stripe patt—134 sts.
Work 4 rows in MC stripe patt—136 sts.
Work 2 rows in CC stripe patt—137 sts.
Work 2 rows in MC stripe patt—138 sts.
Work 2 rows in CC stripe patt—139 sts.
Work 6 rows in MC stripe patt—142 sts.
Work 4 rows in CC stripe patt—144 sts.
Work 2 rows in MC stripe patt—145 sts.
Work 2 rows in CC stripe patt—146 sts.
Work 10 rows in MC stripe patt—151 sts.
Work 4 rows in CC stripe patt—153 sts.
Work 4 rows in MC stripe patt—155 sts.

Work 8 rows in CC stripe patt—159 sts.
Work 2 rows in MC stripe patt—160 sts.
Work 16 rows in CC stripe patt—168 sts.
Work 4 rows in MC stripe patt—170 sts.
Work 8 rows in CC stripe patt—174 sts.
Work 6 rows in MC stripe patt—177 sts.
Work 2 rows in CC stripe patt—178 sts.
Next row: (RS) Work Row 1 of CC stripe patt.
Next row: With CC, loosely bind off knitwise to m, with MC, loosely bind off knitwise to end.

Finishing
Weave in ends. Steam- or wet-block shawl to finished measurements.

Finished measurements
6½" [16.5 cm] wide (8" [20.5 cm] wide at ends) and 52" [132 cm] long

Yarn
Chickadee by Quince & Co
(100% American wool; 181yd [166m]/50g)
- 3 skeins Twig 119

Needles
- One pair in size US 4 [3.5 mm]
- One pair in size US 7 [4.5 mm]

Or size to obtain gauge

Notions
- Locking stitch marker
- Two cable needles (cn)
- Tapestry needle

Gauge
36 sts and 24 rows = 4" [10 cm] in cable panel with larger needles, after blocking.

Special abbreviations
SR (separate rib): Slip next knit st onto cable needle (cn) and hold in front, slip next purl st onto second cn and hold in back, (sl knit st to front cn, sl purl st to back cn) 2 more times.

RR (resume rib): (K1 from front cn, p1 from back cn) 3 times.

T1L (travel rib over 1, leans to the left): SR, k1, then RR.

T1R (travel rib over 1, leans to the right): Slip next st to RH needle, SR, return slipped st to LH needle, RR, then k1.

T2L (travel rib over 2, leans to the left): SR, k2, then RR.

T2R (travel rib over 2, leans to the right): Slip next 2 sts to RH needle, SR, return slipped sts to LH needle, RR, then k2.

T3L (travel rib over 3, leans to the left): SR, k3, then RR.

T3R (travel rib over 3, leans to the right): Slip next 3 sts to RH needle, SR, return slipped sts to LH needle, RR, then k3.

RC12F (rib-cable 6 front, leans to the left): Slip next 6 sts onto cn and hold in front, (k1, p1) 3 times, then (k1, p1) 3 times from cn.

RC12B (rib-cable 6 back, leans to the right): Slip next 6 sts onto cn and hold in back, (k1, p1) 3 times, then (k1, p1) 3 times from cn.

BAROQUE CABLE SCARF, JANUS STYLE
Michael Dworjan

Barbara Walker has been an inspiration to me since I first picked up needles, so I turned to her for a cable pattern to showcase my reversible cable technique, Keyhole Cables. The Baroque Cable is perfect for these cables because the pattern is both complex and full of subtlety.

Cable panel (60 sts)

See also, chart page 67.

Row 1: (RS) K3, (k1, p1) 3 times, k2, (k1, p1) 3 times, k7, (k1, p1) 6 times, k7, (k1, p1) 3 times, k2, (k1, p1) 3 times, k3.

Row 2: Rep Row 1.

Row 3: K3, T1L, T1R, k7, RC12F, k7, T1L, T1R, k3.

Row 4: K4, (k1, p1) 6 times, k8, (k1, p1) 6 times, k8, (k1, p1) 6 times, k4.

Row 5: K4, RC12F, k6, T2R, T2L, k6, RC12F, k4.

Row 6: K4, (k1, p1) 6 times, k6, (k1, p1) 3 times, k4, (k1, p1) 3 times, k6, (k1, p1) 6 times, k4.

Row 7: K4, (k1, p1) 3 times, T1L, k3, T2R, k4, T2L, k3, T1R, (k1, p1) 3 times, k4.

Row 8: K4, (k1, p1) 3 times, k1, (k1, p1) 3 times, k3, (k1, p1) 3 times, k8, (k1, p1) 3 times, k3, (k1, p1) 3 times, k1, (k1, p1) 3 times, k4.

Row 9: K4, T1L, T1L, T2R, k8, T2L, T1R, T1R, k4.

Row 10: K5, (k1, p1) 3 times, k1, (k1, p1) 6 times, k12, (k1, p1) 6 times, k1, (k1, p1) 3 times, k5.

Row 11: K5, T1L, RC12B, k12, RC12B, T1R, k5.

Row 12: K6, (k1, p1) 9 times, k12, (k1, p1) 9 times, k6.

Row 13: K6, RC12F, T3L, k6, T3R, RC12F, k6.

Row 14: K6, (k1, p1) 6 times, k3, (k1, p1) 3 times, k6, (k1, p1) 3 times, k3, (k1, p1) 6 times, k6.

Row 15: K5, T1R, T3L, T3L, T3R, T3R, T1L, k5.

Row 16: K5, (k1, p1) 3 times, k4, (k1, p1) 3 times, k3, (k1, p1) 6 times, k3, (k1, p1) 3 times, k4, (k1, p1) 3 times, k5.

Row 17: K4, T1R, k4, T3L, RC12F, T3R, k4, T1L, k4.

Row 18: K4, (k1, p1) 3 times, k8, (k1, p1) 12 times, k8, (k1, p1) 3 times, k4.

Row 19: K3, T1R, k8, RC12B, RC12B, k8, T1L, k3.

Row 20: K3, (k1, p1) 3 times, k9, (k1, p1) 12 times, k9, (k1, p1) 3 times, k3.

Row 21: K3, (k1, p1) 3 times, k9, (k1, p1) 3 times, RC12F, (k1, p1) 3 times, k9, (k1, p1) 3 times, k3.

Row 22: Rep Row 20.

Row 23: K3, T1L, k8, RC12B, RC12B, k8, T1R, k3.

Row 24: Rep Row 18.

Row 25: K4, T1L, k4, T3R, RC12F, T3L, k4, T1R, k4.

Row 26: Rep Row 16.

Row 27: K5, T1L, T3R, T3R, T3L, T3L, T1R, k5.

Row 28: Rep Row 14.

Row 29: K6, RC12F, T3R, k6, T3L, RC12F, k6.

Row 30: Rep Row 12.

Row 31: K5, T1R, RC12B, k12, RC12B, T1L, k5.

Row 32: Rep Row 10.

Row 33: K4, T1R, T1R, T2L, k8, T2R, T1L, T1L, k4.

Row 34: Rep Row 8.

Row 35: K4, (k1, p1) 3 times, T1R, k3, T2L, k4, T2R, k3, T1L, (k1, p1) 3 times, k4.

Row 36: Rep Row 6.

Row 37: K4, RC12F, k6, T2L, T2R, k6, RC12F, k4.

Row 38: Rep Row 4.

Row 39: K3, T1R, T1L, k7, RC12F, k7, T1R, T1L, k3.

Rows 40-42: Rep Row 1.

Rep Rows 1-42 for cable panel.

Helpful link

For instructions on the **long-tail cast on**, we like: www.knitty.com/ISSUEsummer05/FEATsum-05TT.html

Notes

1. Keyhole Cables allow even the most complex cable patterns to be made reversible without losing any of their subtleties. As a bonus, they also create a very flat fabric—unique in the world of cables.
2. For Keyhole Cables, you divide the knit and purl ribbing stitches onto two cable needles, holding knit stitches in front of work and purl stitches in back. After working the cable as indicated, the ribbing is resumed by alternating knitting one stitch from front and purling one stitch from back cable needles. This creates the keyhole effect—weaving one cable through another—for a reversible fabric.
3. The ends can be fanned out during blocking for a more feminine look.
4. To help distinguish RS from WS in this reversible pattern, after working a few rows, place a locking stitch marker on the RS of scarf.

Scarf

With smaller needles and using the long-tail cast on, CO 60 sts.

Begin trim

First row: (RS) Work Row 1 of cable panel.
Next row: Work Row 2 of patt.
Rep Rows 1 and 2 of patt until scarf meas 5" [12.5 cm] from beg, ending after a WS row. Change to larger needles.

Begin reversible cables

Next row: (RS) Work Row 1 of cable panel.
Cont in patt until Rows 1-42 have been worked a total of 5 times, then rep Rows 1-40 one more time.
Scarf meas approx 47" [119.5 cm] from beg. Change to smaller needles.

Begin trim

Next row: (RS) Work Row 1 of cable panel.
Next row: Work Row 2 of patt.
Work Rows 1 and 2 of patt until trim meas 5" [12.5 cm], ending after a WS row.
Next row: (RS) Loosely bind off purlwise.

Finishing

Weave in ends. Steam-or wet-block scarf to finished measurements.

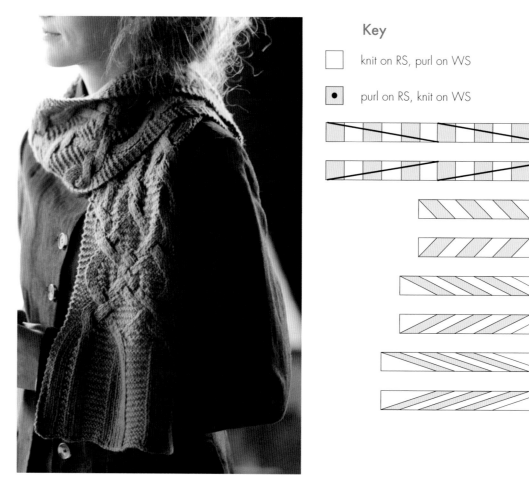

Key

☐ knit on RS, purl on WS

▣ purl on RS, knit on WS

RC12F

RC12B

T1L

T1R

T2L

T2R

T3L

T3R

Baroque cable panel

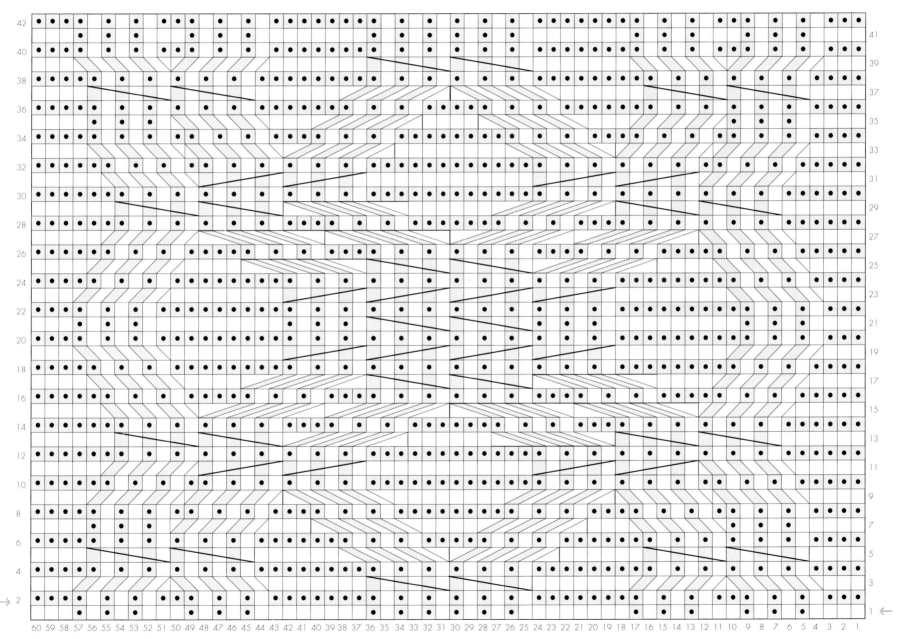

INVERNESS SCARF
Ellie Sokolow

Inverness is a wide, statement scarf with horizontal and vertical stripes and a bold fringe at the ends. Cushy Osprey is a super comfy yarn for wearing around the neck. And its clean colors make it wonderful for the graphic colorwork in this scarf.

Finished measurements
9½" [24 cm] wide and 72½" [184 cm] long, including fringe

Yarn
Osprey by Quince & Co
(100% American wool; 170yd [155m]/100g)
2 skeins
- Slate 143 (A)

1 skein each
- Poppy 140 (B)
- Iceland 153 (C)
- Honey 123 (D)

Needles
- One pair in size US 9 [5.5 mm]

Or size to obtain gauge

Notions
- Locking stitch marker
- Tapestry needle
- Blocking pins and/or wires

Gauge
16 sts and 25 rows = 4" [10 cm] in garter stitch, after wet-blocking, before adding vertical stripes.

Special abbreviations
sl 2 wyif: Slip 2 sts purlwise with yarn in front.
sl 1 wyif: Slip 1 st purlwise with yarn in front.

Garter stitch
Knit every row.

Helpful links
For instructions on the **long-tail cast on**, we like:
www.knitty.com/ISSUEsummer05/FEATsum-05TT.html
For instructions on **duplicate stitch**, we like:
www.knitty.com/ISSUEfall04/FEATfall04TT.html

Notes
1. Scarf is knitted lengthwise in garter stitch and stripe pattern. Lengths of yarn are then drawn through the length of the scarf, creating the vertical stripes and fringe.
2. Edges are worked in an applied i-cord. When changing yarn it isn't necessary to break and rejoin each color. To carry the non-working (travelling) strands along edge of scarf, knit the first stitch with working yarn, then bring the travelling strands up and between the needle and the working yarn and knit the next stitch with working yarn, trapping the travelling strands inside the applied i-cord. Gently tug on the travelling yarn strands, maintaining the scarf's tension. Trap all travelling strands in this manner every RS row. When changing working yarn color, knit the first stitch with new working color and treat the previous working strand as a travelling strand. As you reach the end of the scarf, break each yarn after you work the last row in that color, leaving an 8" [20.5 cm] tail.
3. To help distinguish RS from WS in garter stitch, place a locking stitch marker on the RS of scarf after working a few rows.

Scarf

With A and using the long-tail cast on, CO 37 sts.

First row: (RS) Knit to last 2 sts, sl 2 wyif.
Rep the last row five more times, ending after a WS row.

Begin horizontal stripe pattern

Rows 1 and 2: With B, knit to last 2 sts, sl 2 wyif.
Rows 3 and 4: With C, knit to last 2 sts, sl 2 wyif.
Rows 5 and 6: With B, knit to last 2 sts, sl 2 wyif.
Rows 7-14: With A, knit to last 2 sts, sl 2 wyif.
Rows 15 and 16: With D, knit to last 2 sts, sl 2 wyif.
Row 17-24: With A, knit to last 2 sts, sl 2 wyif.
Rep the last 24 rows 16 more times, then rep Rows 1-12 one more time.
Next row: (RS) Knit to last st, sl 1 wyif.
Next row: Loosely bind off knitwise.

Finishing

Weave in ends using duplicate stitch. Do not cut. Wet-block using pins and/or blocking wires to the following dimensions: 9" [23.5 cm] wide and 74" [188 cm] long. After blocking, trim ends.

Vertical stripes and fringe

To determine the strand lengths for your vertical stripes, measure the length of your finished, blocked scarf, add 12" [30.5 cm] to this measurement, then multiply by 2. Sample scarf used 172" [437 cm] lengths.
Cut six strands of B, three strands of C, and four strands of D, all to the length determined by your scarf's measurement.

First stripe

Thread tapestry needle with one strand of D. Adjust yarn on needle so that the tails are equal length (needle is at center of strand). With RS facing, and beg at the left side of the CO edge, count 4 sts in (2 edge sts and 2 garter sts). Insert tapestry needle under CO edge, then under each garter ridge visible from the RS. Work slowly, 5-7 ridges at a time, stopping to draw the length of yarn through the scarf, gently pulling it, so as not to draw up the garter stitch fabric. Leave approx 6" [15 cm] tail for fringe at CO edge. Work the length of the scarf to BO edge, inserting needle under BO edge. Cut strand, creating two equal lengths approx 6" [15 cm] long.

Next stripe

Thread tapestry needle as established with one strand of C. With RS facing, and beg at CO edge, count 5 sts to the right of last stripe, and work in the same manner as first strand.

Next stripe

Thread tapestry needle as established with one strand of D. With RS facing, and beg at CO edge, count 5 sts to the right of last stripe, and work in the same manner.

Rep the last two stripes two more times. Final stripe in D is located 4 sts from right side of CO edge.

Next stripe

Thread tapestry needle as established with one strand of B. With RS facing, and beg at CO edge, count 1 st to the left of first stripe in C, and work in the same manner.

Next stripe

Thread tapestry needle with one strand of B as established. With RS facing, and beg at CO edge, count 1 st to the right of first stripe in C, and work in the same manner.

Rep the last two stripes two more times. One stripe in B is located on each side of each stripe in C.

All stripes should have even tension on the garter stitch fabric, and each stripe should have two 6" [15 cm] tails each at CO and BO edges. Adjust tension and tail length if necessary by gently drawing excess yarn through the scarf until tails are even.

Secure fringe

Thread both strands of tail from first stripe onto tapestry needle. Insert needle from RS to WS into the st above the CO, looping the tails around the CO, then bring the needle out between the two tails, securing them in place.

Rep for each pair of stripe tails at CO edge, then rep for each stripe at BO edge.
Tie a loose knot into each tail, approx 3½" [9 cm] from the body of the scarf. Tighten once all knots have been made. Trim fringe to the same length, approx 1½" [4 cm] from knots, 5" [12.5 cm] from body of scarf.

SVALBARD COWL

Allison Jane

Svalbard was conceived while I was still living in Maine; an attempt to make a neck covering thick and warm enough to combat the snow and winds. Svalbard fits the bill just right! It's big enough to wear pulled down over the shoulders, even when wearing a chunky winter coat.

Finished measurements
33¼" [84.5 cm] upper circumference,
43" [109 cm] lower circumference,
14" [35.5 cm] deep

Yarn
Puffin by Quince & Co
(100% American wool; 112yd [102m]/100g)
- 4 skeins Sedum 142

Needles
- One 32" circular needle in size US 15 [10 mm]

Or size to obtain gauge

Notions
- Stitch marker
- Cable needle (cn)
- Tapestry needle

Gauge
13 sts and 17 rnds = 4" [10 cm] in stockinette stitch, after blocking.

Special abbreviations
k1/R (right lifted increase): Pick up the right leg of the st below the next st on LH needle and knit it, then knit the next stitch (1 st increased).

ssk (slip, slip, knit): Slip 2 sts one at a time knitwise to the RH needle; return sts to LH needle in turned position and knit them together through the back loops (1 st decreased, leans to the left).

k2tog: Knit 2 sts together (1 st decreased, leans to the right).

C10B (cable 10 back, leans to the right): Slip next 5 sts onto cable needle (cn) and hold in back, k5, then k5 from cn.

C10F (cable 10 front, leans to the left): Slip next 5 sts onto cn and hold in front, k5, then k5 from cn.

C4/5R (cross 4 over 5, right): Slip next 5 sts onto cn and hold in back, k4, then k5 from cn.

C4/5L (cross 4 over 5, left): Slip next 4 sts onto cn and hold in front, k5, then k4 from cn.

C8F (cable 8 front, leans to the left): Slip next 4 sts onto cn and hold in front, k4, then k4 from cn.

C8B (cable 8 back, leans to the right): Slip next 4 sts onto cn and hold in back, k4, then k4 from cn.

Stockinette stitch (St st)
Knit every round.

Helpful link
For instructions on the **long-tail cast on**, we like: www.knitty.com/ISSUEsummer05/FEATsum05TT.html

Notes
1. Cowl is knitted in the round, from the bottom, with decreases occurring between cable sections to shape.
2. The first row is worked flat, so purl side of the cast on will be on the RS of cowl. Last round is bound off purlwise, to match beginning.

Cowl

Begin at lower edge

Using the long-tail cast on, CO 140 sts. Do not join.

Begin rib trim

First row: (RS) *K1, p1; rep from * to end. Place marker for beg of rnd and join to work in the rnd, being careful not to twist sts.

Next rnd: *K1, p1; rep from *.

Work in rib as est for 2 more rnds.

Begin body

Next rnd *inc rnd*: K2, k1/R, k1, k1/R, *k3, k1/R; rep from * to last 3 sts, k1, k1/R, k1 (36 sts inc'd)—176 sts.

Work 5 rnds even in St st.

Next rnd: *K1, C10B, k1, C10F; rep from *.

Work 10 rnds even in St st.

Next rnd: *K1, C10F, k1, C10B; rep from *.

Work 15 rnds even in St st.

Next rnd *dec rnd*: *K4, ssk, k11, k2tog, k3; rep from * to end (16 sts dec'd)—160 sts rem.

Next rnd: *K1, C4/5R, k1, C4/5L; rep from *.

Work 9 rnds even in St st.

Next rnd *dec rnd*: *K4, k2tog, k9, ssk, k3; rep from * to end (16 sts dec'd)—144 sts rem.

Next rnd: *K1, C8F, k1, C8B; rep from *.

Work 5 rnds even in St st.

Next rnd *dec rnd*: *K2, k2tog; rep from * to end (36 sts dec'd)—108 sts rem.

Begin rib trim

Next rnd: *K1, p1; rep from *.

Work in rib as est for 2 more rnds.

Next rnd: Bind off purlwise.

Finishing

Weave in ends. Steam- or wet-block cowl to finished measurements.

WENDING COWL

Quenna Lee

Wending is an infinity cowl with a meandering lace stripe to provide the visual interest. This is a quick project with varied components—a bit of lace and short rows. Owl, textured and heathered, warm yet lofty, provides a soft earthiness to this accessory.

Finished measurements
52¼" [132.5 cm] circumference and 8" [20 cm] deep

Yarn
Owl by Quince & Co
(50% American wool, 50% alpaca; 120yd [110m]/50g)
- 3 skeins Abyssinian 309

Needles
- One 32" circular needle in size US 8 [5 mm]

Or size to obtain gauge

Notions
- Stitch marker
- Tapestry needle

Gauge
17 sts and 26 rnds = 4" [10 cm] in stockinette stitch, after blocking.

Special abbreviations
k2tog: Knit 2 sts together (1 st decreased, leans to the right).

ssk (slip, slip, knit): Slip 2 sts one at a time knit-wise to the RH needle; return sts to LH needle in turned position and knit them together through the back loops (1 st decreased, leans to the left).

yo (yarn over): Bring yarn between needles to the front, then over RH needle ready to knit the next st (1 st increased).

m1 (make 1): Insert LH needle from front to back under horizontal strand between st just worked and the next st, knit lifted strand through the back loop (1 st increased).

w&t (wrap and turn):
(RS) Slip next st to the RH needle and bring yarn between needles to the front of work. Return slipped st to the LH needle. Turn work and bring yarn between needles to front, ready to work next WS row.
(WS) Slip next st to the RH needle and bring yarn between needles to the back of the work. Return slipped st to the LH needle. Turn work and bring yarn between needles to back, ready to work next RS row.

Stockinette stitch (St st)
Knit every round.

Garter ridge and lace pattern (multiple of 17 sts)
See also chart, page 74.
Rnd 1: Purl.
Rnd 2: *(K2tog) three times, (yo, k1) five times, yo, (ssk) three times; rep from * to end.
Rnds 3 and 4: Knit.
Rnd 5: Purl.
Rnds 6-8: Knit.
Rep Rnds 1–8 for garter ridge and lace pattern.

Techniques
Picking up wraps
(RS) Insert the right needle tip into the wrap from below, front to back, then into the stitch that it wraps, and knit the two together, making sure that the wrap falls to the wrong side of the work.
(WS) Insert the right needle tip into the wrap from below, back to front, lifting it over the stitch that it wraps, and purl the two together, making sure that the wrap falls to the wrong side of work.

Helpful links

For instructions on the **long-tail cast on**, we like:
www.knitty.com/ISSUEsummer05/FEATsum-05TT.html
For additional information on **wrap-and-turn short rows**, see:
www.knitty.com/ISSUEsummer03/FEATbonnet-ric.html

Note

Cowl is worked from the bottom up in the round. The wavy garter and lace pattern is formed with short rows.

Cowl

Using the long-tail cast on, loosely CO 222 sts. Place marker for beg of rnd and join to work in the rnd, being careful not to twist sts.

Begin rib trim at lower edge

First rnd: *K1, p1; rep from * to end.
Rep the last rnd one more time.
Work 2 rnds in St st.
Next rnd: *P1, k1; rep from *.
Rep the last rnd one more time.
Work 4 rnds in St st.

Begin short rows

Next row *short row 1:* (RS) K74, w&t;
(WS) p148, w&t.
Next row *short row 2:* (RS) Knit to 7 sts before wrapped st, w&t; (WS) purl to 7 sts before wrapped st, w&t.
Rep *short row 2* seven more times.
Next row: (RS) Knit to end, picking up wraps. Begin working in the rnd.

Begin lace stripe

Next rnd *dec rnd:* K2tog, knit to end, picking up wraps (1 st dec'd)—221 sts rem.
Next rnd: Work Rnd 1 of garter ridge and lace patt.
Cont as est until Rnds 1-8 of patt have been worked a total of two times, then work Rnds 1-5 one more time.
Next rnd: Knit.

Begin short row shaping

Next row *short row 1:* (RS) K149, w&t;
(WS) p76, w&t.
Next row *short row 2:* (RS) Knit to wrapped st, pick up wrap, k6, w&t; (WS) purl to wrapped st, pick up wrap, p6, w&t.
Rep *short row 2* seven more times.
Next row: (RS) Knit to end, picking up last wrap. Begin working in the rnd.
Next rnd *inc rnd:* M1, knit to end, picking up last wrap (1 st inc'd)—222 sts.
Work 4 rnds in St st.

Begin rib trim

First rnd: *K1, p1; rep from * to end.
Rep the last rnd one more time.
Work 2 rnds in St st.
Next rnd: *P1, k1; rep from *.
Rep the last rnd one more time.
Next rnd: Bind off as follows: K1, *yo, k1, sl 2 sts to BO, k1, sl 1 st to BO; rep from * to end. Break yarn and draw through rem st.

Finishing

Weave in ends. Steam- or wet-block cowl to finished measurements.

Key

☐	knit
⊡	purl
⊙	yo
◩	k2tog
◪	ssk

Garter ridge and lace pattern

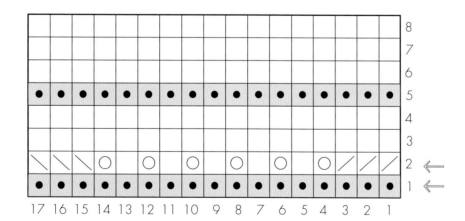

TWIST OF FATE

Laura Reinbach

I am fascinated by the endless possibilities of creating texture in knitting. It's amazing to me how manipulating stitches in various ways can create such unique and beautiful patterns. This scarf is just one example. It is created by twisting stitches so they slant one way and then the other. The wrong side is interesting and lovely in its own right.

Finished measurements
11" [28 cm] wide and 78" [198 cm] long
Yarn
Chickadee by Quince & Co
(100% American wool; 181yd [166m]/50g)
- 7 skeins Clay 113
Needles
- One pair in size US 5 [3.75 mm]
Or size to obtain gauge
Notions
- Stitch markers (m)
- Tapestry needle
Gauge
27 sts and 39 rows = 4" [10 cm] in twisted stitch panel, before wet-blocking
32 sts and 32 rows = 4" [10 cm] in twisted stitch panel, after wet-blocking.

Special abbreviations
LT (left twist): Skip 1 st and knit the next st through the back, keeping both sts on needle, knit the 2 sts together, then slip both sts from needle.
RT (right twist): K2tog leaving sts on LH needle, knit first st again, then slip both sts from needle.

Twisted stitch panel (78 sts)
See also chart, pages 78 and 79.
Row 1: (RS) K1, (LT) six times, (RT) seven times, p4, (RT) seven times, LT, p4, (LT) six times, (RT) seven times, k1.
Row 2: P26, k5, p16, k5, p26.
Row 3: K2, (LT) five times, (RT) seven times, p4, (RT) seven times, (LT) two times, p4, (LT) five times, (RT) seven times, k2.
Row 4: P25, k5, p18, k5, p25.
Row 5: K3, (LT) four times, (RT) seven times, p4, (RT) seven times, (LT) three times, p4, (LT) four times, (RT) seven times, k3.
Row 6: P24, k5, p20, k5, p24.
Row 7: K4, (LT) three times, (RT) seven times, p4, (RT) seven times, (LT) four times, p4, (LT) three times, (RT) seven times, k4.
Row 8: P23, k5, p22, k5, p23.
Row 9: K5, (LT) two times, (RT) seven times, p4, (RT) seven times, (LT) five times, p4, (LT) two times, (RT) seven times, k5.
Row 10: P22, k5, p24, k5, p22.
Row 11: K6, LT, (RT) seven times, p4, (RT) seven times, (LT) six times, p4, LT, (RT) seven times, k6.
Row 12: P21, k5, p26, k5, p21.
Row 13: K7, (RT) seven times, p4, (RT) seven times, (LT) seven times, p4, (RT) seven times, k7.
Row 14: Rep Row 12.
Row 15: K6, (RT) seven times, LT, p4, (LT) six times, (RT) seven times, p4, (RT) seven times, LT, k6.
Row 16: Rep Row 10.
Row 17: K5, (RT) seven times, (LT) two times, p4, (LT) five times, (RT) seven times, p4, (RT) seven times, (LT) two times, k5.
Row 18: Rep Row 8.

Row 19: K4, (RT) seven times, (LT) three times, p4, (LT) four times, (RT) seven times, p4, (RT) seven times, (LT) three times, k4.

Row 20: Rep Row 6.

Row 21: K3, (RT) seven times, (LT) four times, p4, (LT) three times, (RT) seven times, p4, (RT) seven times, (LT) four times, k3.

Row 22: Rep Row 4.

Row 23: K2, (RT) seven times, (LT) five times, p4, (LT) two times, (RT) seven times, p4 (RT) seven times, (LT) five times, k2.

Row 24: Rep Row 2.

Row 25: K1, (RT) seven times, (LT) six times, p4, LT, (RT) seven times, p4, (RT) seven times, (LT) six times, k1.

Row 26: P27, k5, p14, k5, p27.

Row 27: (RT) seven times, (LT) seven times, p4, (RT) seven times, p4, (RT) seven times, (LT) seven times.

Row 28: Rep Row 26.

Rep Rows 1-28 for twisted stitch panel.

Helpful link

For instructions on the **cable cast on**, we like: www.knitty.com/ISSUEsummer05/FEATsum-05TT.html

Notes

1. Scarf is knitted flat, lengthwise, with a ribbed border.
2. Please note the difference in the working gauge and the blocked gauge. Wet-blocking (as opposed to steam-blocking) is recommended to achieve drape and proper gauge. Your scarf will stretch in length and shrink slightly in width during the blocking process.

Scarf

Using the cable cast on, CO 90 sts.

Begin rib trim

First row: (RS) *K1, p1; rep from * to end.
Work in rib as est until pc meas 1" [2.5 cm] from beg, ending after a WS row.

Begin twisted stitch panel

Next row: (RS) (K1, p1) three times, place marker (pm), work Row 1 of twisted st panel to last 6 sts, pm, (k1, p1) three times to end.

Next row: Work in rib to marker (m), work next row of patt to next m, work in rib to end.
Cont as est, working Rows 1-28 of patt until pc meas approx 72" [183 cm], ending after Row 14 or 28.

Begin rib trim

Next row: (RS) *K1, p1; rep from * to end.
Work in rib as est for 1" [2.5 cm].

Next row: Bind off in pattern.

Finishing

Weave in ends. Wet-block scarf to finished measurements.

Key

☐ knit on RS, purl on WS

▪ purl on RS, knit on WS

⊘ RT

⊗ LT

Twisted stitch panel, stitches 39-78

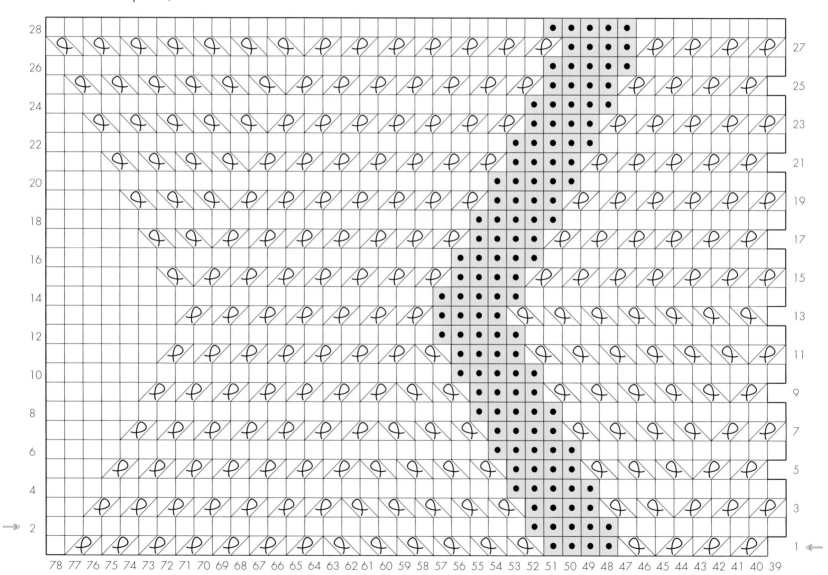

Twisted stitch panel, stitches 1-39

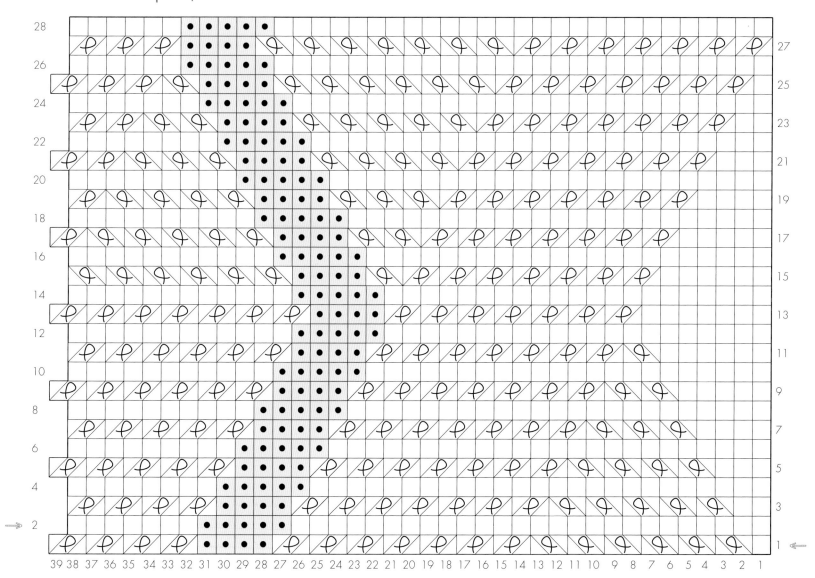

Standard Abbreviations

approx	approximately		p	purl
beg	begin(ning); begin; begins		patt(s)	pattern(s)
BO	bind off		pc(s)	piece(s)
BOR	beginning of round		pm	place marker
CO	cast on		psso	pass slipped stitch(es) over
CC	contrasting color		rem	remain(ing)
circ	circular needle		rep	repeat; repeating
cm	centimeter(s)		RH	right hand
cn	cable needle		rib	ribbing
cont	continue(s); continuing		rnd(s)	round(s)
dec('d)	decrease(d)		RS	right side
est	establish(ed)		sl	slip
g	gram(s)		sl m	slip marker
inc('d)	increase(d)		st(s)	stitch(es)
k	knit		St st	stockinette stitch
LH	left hand		tog	together
MC	main color		wyib	with yarn in back
meas	measures		wyif	with yarn in front
mm	millimeter(s)		WS	wrong side
m(s)	marker(s)		yd	yard(s)

Shannon Squire

I am completely and totally addicted to knitting. I have at least a bazillion projects on the needles at any one time, and am always dreaming up new designs. I've been designing since 2010, and have been published in Knitty.com, Quince & Co, and the Blue Moon Fiber Arts Rockin' Sock Club, as well as in oodles of Twisted Yarn Shop clubs and ebooks. I have two wee gals (Hazel, born in 2009 and Astrid, born in 2011), so my days are full of purple and Matchbox cars and My Little Ponies and Dinosaurs, as well as fiber and swatching and casting on. You can buy my patterns on Ravelry or Craftsy.com, or through Ravelry's In-Store Pattern Sales program throughout the 'verse.

website: gatheringwoolinpdx.com
on Ravelry: shannon

Amy Maceyko

I am an architect in Pittsburgh with a strong crafty nature. I had thought for years about designing knit and crochet patterns, but it wasn't until the recession threw me into unemployment that I began to write down my improvised designs. I've also taught at my LYS and at a regional festival for three years before finally getting my architectural career back on track. I continue to design in my spare time, and named my Ravelry store *Structured Stitches* because I love thinking about the ways in which knit and crochet patterns, constructions and shapes have similarities to architecture.

In addition to self-published patterns available on Ravelry, I have a design in *60 Quick Knits from America's Yarn Shops*, and three patterns slated for the Cooperative Press Series Fresh Designs Crochet. My designs are also featured in kits sold by Ross Farm Fibers of Washington, Pennsylvania, using yarn made from their Heritage and Rare Breed flock of sheep.

blog and website: structuredstitches.wordpress.com
on Ravelry: PghAmers

Katherine Mehls

My grandmother Beryl Maud Foreman Day taught me to crochet when I was little. Soon after, I taught myself to knit from a book. Years later, my friend Sunday Holm taught me how to navigate the knitting world. I combine my love of knitwear, design, and photography in working for my LYS and also photographing for local designers. I have designs for Sixth & Spring Books due out in 2015. This is my first pattern for Quince & Co.

website: cloudknitting.com
on Ravelry: MizKay

Noriko Ho

Ever since I was a kid, I've had a passion for a variety of things. Math, science, art, and crafts are all things I truly enjoy. However, it wasn't until I discovered knitting that I truly discovered an outlet for all of my creativity. I love the rhythmic feel of the yarn and needles, and how tangible the results are. Designing has allowed me to further my creativity and express what I envision in my head. I am currently living with my boyfriend, Bret, and my little kitty, Izi. When I'm not working or crafting, I love reading and trying new foods and restaurants. I also enjoy spinning, dyeing yarn, and going on yarn crawls with some of my best friends.

blog: norichanknits.blogspot.com
on Ravelry: norichan

Makiho Negishi

I was born and grew up in Japan. I learned crochet and knitting from my mother at the age of 10. I designed and knitted my first original sweater at the age of 17. After marriage, Ravelry gave me an opportunity to knit more overseas patterns. The overseas knitting technique is wonderful and interesting. I would like to enjoy carrying out a creative activity from now on.

blog: kero5963.blogspot.jp
on Ravelry: bullfr0g

Deb Hoss

I studied painting in college, and over the years I've worked with photography and fashion, made art books, raised my daughter, held challenging employment, and, throughout, have also knitted. Since 2010 I've focused all of my creative attention on knitwear design. The internet has made this work possible and I'm grateful for that. My sweaters tend to be slim, shaped, minimal and unfussy. I like to look for the threads in life that perhaps carry through generations. These days my daughter Juliet is my model (and my muse), and I spend my days designing, knitting, and writing—happily. I love to mine my family lore and name my patterns for those who came before me and their stories.

blog: debhossknits.blogspot.com
website: debhossknits.com
on Ravelry: debhoss

Melissa "Mel" Schoenwether

I live, breathe and love ohana, the ocean and knitting. After many years on the islands of Oah'u and Kaua'i, my knitting designs have strong ties to salt water, the land and nature. My knitting life began on a different island in south east Alaska, in the town of Sitka. I had the great fortune to be completely bedridden during a pregnancy…the silver lining being private daily lessons 6 days a week from an accomplished Swedish knitter, who taught me to knit and purl, do lace and cables, bobbles and entrelac, and thereby saved my sanity and gave me an entirely new medium to love nature and people through. You can find me creating and sharing on my blog.

blog: withmeldotcom.wordpress.com
on Ravelry: MSkiKnits

Michael Dworjan

I am a knitwear designer from NYC, NY who specializes in reversibility, double-knitting, and interesting constructions. I am known for my inventions in double-knit lace, reversible cables, and asymmetrical shawls. I have been published in Love of Knitting, Vogue Knitting, and I Like Knitting. Always interested in meeting other knitters, I am a member of several local knitting groups and always seeking more through Ravelry.

website: aptenoknits.com
on Ravelry: Aptenoknits

Angela Tong

I am a knit and crochet designer living in New Jersey with my husband, two daughters, and a dog named Caesar. My designs have been published in books and magazines. I enjoy teaching others how to weave, knit, and crochet. You can find my online weaving class at Craftsy.com, and my shawl dvd and pin-loom video on the Interweave Press website. As a lifelong crafter, I have never met a craft I didn't like.

blog: angelatong.blogspot.com
on Ravelry: AngelaTong

Ellie Sokolow

I live in New Mexico with my husband and our chocolate lab. I studied art history and now work as a photographer and graphic designer. At age six, I learned to knit from a family friend who helped me make a pink garter stitch scarf for my teddy bear. When not working or knitting, I enjoy growing orchids, gardening, and hiking.

website: elliesokolow.com
on Ravelry: elliesok

Allison Jane

I am (currently) a Texas-based knits designer because nothing says fun like sitting under a pile of wool in 110°F heat. I am an avid traveler and a member of the mile-high knitting club. I have yet to finish one of those knitted honeycomb quilts despite obsessively knitting little yarn pockets at the bar.

website: allisonjaneknits.com
Ravelry: Allison Jane

Quenna Lee

After designing and producing fabric wallets and handbags at Blissful on Etsy, I rediscovered knitting. Tired of constantly reworking patterns, I began designing my own garments, with an emphasis on top-down construction, clean lines, and flattering silhouettes. I am based in Northern California. My work has appeared in Knitscene, Interweave Knits, Knit Picks, Knit.Wear, and Twist Collective.

website: blissfulbyquenna.com
on Ravelry: blissful

Laura Reinbach

I am a native Floridian who now resides in a small town in Maine with my husband and four boys. Although I may complain of the cold from time to time, I am very grateful to wear my knitted items most of the year. I was taught to knit by my mother-in-law after my first son was born. I was quite slow at first and didn't become an avid knitter until I discovered Ravelry a few years ago. Now I am obsessed and there is no turning back. Recently, I have become interested in creating my own knitwear and have started to dabble in the design process.

on Ravelry: Lulubach

Quince & Company makes beautiful yarns in natural fibers. We spin our yarns primarily in New England from wool sourced from American sheep. We began in 2010 with four classic, wool yarns in weights from sport to chunky, each dyed in 37 colors. Today we make eight different yarns in the United States and import two organic linen yarns from Italy. We ship our yarns all over the world—from Tazmania to Korea to Brazil. Find out more about us at www.quinceandco.com.

We'd like to thank everyone who took the time and made the effort to submit an idea for this year's scarf collection. Any book that would include them all would have to be hundreds of pages long. The hardest step in creating this collection each year is choosing which scarves, cowls, and shawls to include from the many sent in.

Thanks, too, to the designer/knitters of this year's collection for their strong designs and careful craftsmanship.

In addition, we'd like to thank:

Bliss Boutiques in Portland, Maine, for their help with stylng. You can see what they currently have on offer at blissboutiques.com;

Garry Bowcott at Salvage BBQ, for letting us set up and shoot before hours, several mornings running;

Nyanen Deng and Kathleen Milliken for modeling;

and to Jerusha Robinson, Dawn Catanzaro, and Karen Martinez, whose help in technical editing, proofing, and every other little thing it takes to bring off a project like this is invaluable.